Daylight for the Soul

Daylight for the Soul

A Guide for Finding Peace in Everyday Living

Elizabeth Pelkey

ISBN-13: 9781978190726
ISBN-10: 1978190727
Library of Congress Control Number: 2017915987
CreateSpace Independent Publishing Platform
North Charleston, South Carolina

Contents

Preface

❖ ❖ ❖

CONTINUE—OR EMBARK ON—YOUR spiritual journey with fifty-two meditations gleaned from the spiritual masters. Their insights will inspire you as you reflect on your own life and the ways you can more fully embrace love over fear. Each selection is designed to move you forward on your path to living in peace.

We are all on our own spiritual journeys; no one person's path is identical to another's. Yet we all have much in common. We all succumb to fear at times. We all struggle with accepting reality as it is and ourselves as we are. And we all strive to increase our abilities to center our lives and our choices from a place of love.

Three years were spent gathering and meditating on these teachings channeled from the spiritual masters. Allow these fifty-two meditations to help you on your own journey. The topics are organized alphabetically but can be read in whatever order you deem most helpful. Consult your own inner guidance.

Ask yourself: How does this topic apply to me and my life at this moment? Use the space available following each entry to note what emotions you are feeling, be they positive or negative, and any memories that come during reflection or meditation. Write down what comes to mind without too much thought. Your first thought, vision, or feeling usually comes from your soul and is what you are ready to address.

Delve into this book, put its words into practice, and you may find that fear loosens its grip and you are able to more fully live your life from a place of love and peace within.

Acceptance

❖ ❖ ❖

WHY IS IT so difficult to accept yourself for who you are? Why is it that you seek acceptance from everyone around you, yet sometimes fail to seek it from the most important person—you? The only acceptance you need is the acceptance of your own heart, your own mind, your own body, your own soul. That is all. Accept and love yourself for who you are, and you will no longer seek acceptance outside of yourself. Acceptance, gratitude, and love can all be found within.

Remember, any positive emotion found from within can never be taken from you, and it is not dependent on anything external. The way to acceptance and the way to self-love is from within. Begin by accepting that which is easiest to accept and believe. Maybe it is your natural talent, maybe it is your intelligence, maybe it is your athleticism, maybe it is your creativity, maybe it is your sense of humor, maybe it is your work ethic, maybe it is your health—whatever it is, accept what is easy to accept first. Then this acceptance can be built upon, layer by layer, as you look deep within at who you are—who you really are. Not how others see you, but how you see yourself.

How do you talk to yourself? Do you say kind words about yourself, or are you self-critical? Self-criticism will do more damage to the soul than any words from another. Why? Because your own words never leave you until you let them go. They will play through your mind and your heart and your soul forever if you let them. It is up to you to silence the words of self-doubt, self-loathing, and self-hatred and replace them with words of encouragement, acceptance, and love.

Again, start with what you truly believe is worthy of acceptance. Each and every soul is equipped with gifts and strengths that are brought into this lifetime just for times when they are needed most. Take the time to evaluate who you are and what makes you unique and what is easy to accept about yourself. Begin at the beginning and, one by one, begin accepting each and every part of yourself. Then you may get to the place where you can no longer accept yourself, and where the negative and hurtful words come in, and you feel lost and abandoned and unlovable. This is where healing is needed, and this is where you can begin.

The path to acceptance begins with that which you find unacceptable. That which you cannot stand about yourself. That which you find unlovable. This is where you begin healing, and healing will bring you to acceptance, and acceptance will bring you to love, and love will bring you to peace. Begin healing today and find your way to accept, love, and be at peace with all the parts of you—not just the strengths and gifts, but your weaknesses and shadows, too. They are all a part of you and must eventually be accepted and loved in order for you to find the peace you seek.

Reflection

Attachment to People and Objects

⸻ ❖ ❖ ❖ ⸻

WHAT DOES ATTACHMENT mean to you? Is it attaching yourself to a person? To an object? To a goal? To an outcome? Attachment is a pattern found in all souls and begins in the womb. The embryo is attached to the mother, and so it begins. Attachment then plays an important role in making human connection, so it is no surprise that it becomes a pattern.

For the most part, attachment brings with it rewards of connection, belonging, having someone or something that can bring some kind of comfort and stability to your life. Attachment, however, is not ownership, is not guaranteed, and is not always healthy, and it is important to think about the attachments in your life. You may be attached to your family; however, is this attachment helping you to grow independently or holding you to old ideas that don't fit you anymore?

You see, attachment can bring stagnation—a stalling of sorts in the development of your own beliefs, your own desires, your own adventures outside of your family. As you expand your awareness, it is important to begin to detach from the need to be attached to someone. You can still love, you can still be a part of someone's life, the bond will still be there, but the need will become a want once you let go of the attachment.

Attachment to objects can bring both joy and pain. What objects are you attached to? Do they bring you memories of happiness and joy, or despair and pain? Many times, humans hold onto objects from the past that only keep them rooted in the past and unable to move forward in the present. Take stock of the objects you are attached to and ask yourself if these objects evoke pleasant or painful memories. Let go of any object that does not elicit a positive emotion. One can become bound instead of attached to memories of the past, and being bound does not promote freedom within. Free yourself from the binds of attachment, and instead be connected through your thoughts, your feelings, your actions, and your reactions to the people and objects in your life.

Reflection

Attachment to Goals and Outcomes

————— ❖ ❖ ❖ —————

As FOR ATTACHMENT to goals and outcomes: Let go. If one is attached to a goal and not the process of discovery, isn't the goal lost anyway? Then the goal just becomes a means to an end, to an outcome. It is perfectly healthy to have goals, although some you may outgrow but doggedly hold onto because they are comfortable even though they do not fit anymore. Reevaluate your goals and see which ones still make sense to your heart—not your mind, but your heart.

Do you feel attachment, or do you feel free? Free to make changes in the goals you seek? Do not be bound by your attachment to goals that you no longer feel are necessary to your life.

As for attachment to outcomes: Let go. Let go. Let go. Outcomes become expectations, and expectations often become disappointments. When you are attached to an outcome, you can become so focused on it that you do not see the other opportunities in front of you. Begin to see the fulfillment, the joy that can be found in the journey, the experience, and, most important, the process of allowing.

Allow yourself to detach from those who bind you, allow yourself to detach from objects that do not bring you warmth, detach from goals that no longer suit you, and let go of all outcomes and expectations. Allow those you love to flow in and out of your life. Allow objects to go, along with the negative memories attached to them; allow goals to alter, or to not exist if they no longer fit; and do not allow outcomes to keep you from enjoying what and who comes in to your life.

Reflection

Balance

———— ❖ ❖ ❖ ————

WHY IS IT so hard to achieve balance in your life? Why is it so hard to find the balance between body, mind, and spirit, between work, play, and living your life? Why is so hard to find the balance you seek in what you eat or don't eat, how much money you make or don't make, how much time you have for what is important, and how much time you give to that which is not?

Finding life balance is critical to soul growth, not to mention finding joy and ultimately peace in your life. Finding balance sometimes feels like an eternal search for the Holy Grail. Does it even exist? Is it actually feasible? Is it even possible? Those who say they have found balance—have they really? Is it something that is even attainable? Is it something to strive for?

The answer is yes, absolutely, and you are doing yourself a disfavor by not trying. Simply the act of trying to find balance will lead you to the balance you seek. Look within for the answers you seek, look within for the guidance you need to achieve balance in your life. Balance is not control, by the way, which is what many of you may think. If only I could control where my time goes, if only I could control what I spend my time on, if only I could control who I see and who I do not—if only, if only, if only.

Do you not realize by now that you can choose, which is far different than control? You make conscious choices every day, many choices, actual choices that affect the balance of your everyday life. Have you said yes when you really wanted to say no? Have you done something today that could really have waited until tomorrow or did not even have to be done in the first place? How much time are you wasting doing what you think will please others, only to displease yourself?

Once you figure out that you have all the time you need for balance within a twenty-four-hour day, you will come to realize that saying no to someone else may in fact be saying yes to yourself. Far from being selfish, saying no is actually allowing the balance in and allowing this sense of balance and peace to saturate your soul. This will allow you more time: more time to share your love with others, more time to spend with those you love and those who truly need your guiding hand. Saying no is actually a way to balance yourself, to find that balance you seek.

So why are you afraid to say no? Reframe your thinking and see that it is not really saying no, but actually saying yes to *you*. Practice saying yes to yourself, and you will see that saying yes is the first and most important step toward finding the balance within your own mind, body, and ultimately your soul. Find the time, for it is there. Find the courage to say no, for it is necessary. Find the strength to say yes to what you need so you can find the balance in your life.

Elizabeth Pelkey

Reflection

Being. Existing. Living.

———————— ❖ ❖ ❖ ————————

ARE THEY ALL the same, or is one greater than the other? Human beings are always in a state of being, of existing, but is this really living? Is this simply breathing? Are you really living and fulfilling not only your dreams, but your purpose? It is one's purpose in life that defines a life. It is one's life that deserves a beginning, a middle, and an end. If you fulfill your purpose, is this when you die? Or is it simply of another way of living?

Death is life and life is death; they are one and the same. Don't be afraid of dying, be afraid of not living—truly living—in your soul purpose. Walk, talk, sleep, dream, and live your soul's purpose—the path that everyone seeks without knowing, the path that every awakened soul knows exists and wants so desperately to find. It is right there in front of you. You can only see it once you break down the walls that have been built around you. Once you let go of the trappings of the earthly world.

Once you let go, let go of control, let go of simply "being," will you find the path—the path to your soul, of your soul—and this path will always lead to an awareness that you must help others. You must be the light, not the darkness. The darkness must leave your life in order for you to find your path. You can only find the path with your light, and only your light will open the path for others—not to follow you, but to find their own unique path and their own unique life.

It is when one finds the purpose of the soul that one will find peace, and the most important peace, that of within. It cannot be gained from outside the soul; it must be from within. Peace is only peace when it is created by the soul, for the soul, with the soul, and simply for the purpose of bringing peace to others and peace to the world.

So, find your path, find your path to peace, and find your path to inner peace. We need each and every one of you to be at peace so that the earth can be healed and all can become one. Begin truly living today, and go in search of what your soul knows is there but must be sought to be found. Peace.

Reflection

Belief

❖ ❖ ❖

WHAT IS IT that you believe? What is it that you hold to be true, to be self-evident? What is it that you live your life by? What tenets do you follow? What rules do you believe in? What truths touch your soul? These are questions you must ask yourself as you follow your soul's path. Others cannot answer these questions for you; they must be answered by you and you alone.

What, exactly, do you believe? Has this belief been tested? Has this belief changed with time, with maturity, with wisdom, with soul growth? What do you believe with your soul? Not what someone else tells you to believe, but what *you* believe. This is what is important. It is time for you to stop following and start leading your own life, your own journey, your own path, your own soul. Stop following and start leading.

Why is it that so many of you are afraid to lead and prefer to be led? Why is it that you believe someone else has a closer relationship with the divine than you do? Why? Is it because you do not feel worthy enough to communicate with the divine? You are and you can, but first you must believe, you must believe in something, in something. It does not matter what you believe. It does matter for you to begin to see the similarities between each other and not the differences. Then there will be peace; then and only then will there be peace.

So today, question your own beliefs. If you believe in someone or something that tells you that you are more special than someone else, or that you should pity someone else because he or she does not believe what you do, then your soul has not reached the level of divine love. It is imperative that you follow this truth, that you have the guiding principles of acceptance in your life, that you treat others with respect, that you include *all* others, not just those who are just like you. That you open your arms and welcome *all* others. That you do not look down upon others because they do not believe as you do.

Why do you think that your beliefs are more important than someone else's? That you have all the knowledge? That you have all the answers, or that your particular form of worship is all that there is? Why? Why? Why? It is such an individual choice, and there is absolutely no difference. What you so desperately want is to be at peace with yourself. Then you can truly begin to help others. Then you can truly be a beacon of light for others, and then you can truly be one with the divine. So, question what it is that you believe. Is it love? Is it respect? Is it acceptance? If so, then you will find peace.

Elizabeth Pelkey

Reflection

Centered on Self versus Self-Centered

To be centered on self is not to be self-centered; that is an antiquated notion that is put upon humans by their society, particularly American society. To be centered on self means that you fill your own cup before you fill another's, as you cannot give from an empty vessel. If you are in service to your own soul, to the heart-centered space within, then when you center on yourself, you open yourself up to your own authentic self without pretense, without rebuke, without judgment, but with love, compassion, and acceptance.

To get to this place of acceptance, you must spend time in solitude, even if for just a short period every day. In solitude, you can center your thoughts and feelings on yourself and begin to heal from within, to begin to understand from within, begin to know yourself and what you want, what will fulfill you from a heart space full of love and not fear. You see, this is the key difference. It is important that you begin to know the difference between the two.

For example, if you are being pulled in all directions by family, job, and personal responsibilities, isn't it most self-loving to give yourself something to soothe your soul? Isn't it coming from a place of love if you say, "not now" and give yourself time to rest? There are so many moments that you can do this, even if your life seems overwhelming. Just soothing your soul for five minutes alone in a space that is peaceful will do.

Many of you have the time, but you are afraid others will question, will think you are being self-centered. Being self-centered is when you come from a place of fear. If I don't do this for someone, he or she won't like me, or if I don't immediately call this person back, he or she will think I am mad—you see fear here, yes? You are afraid someone will withdraw affection if you are not there for every request. Then why not be there for yourself?

You and your love are of the utmost importance—your love of self. Your love of yourself. Yes. You read this correctly: your love of self is even more important than your love of your children or your spouse or your parents. You know why: because if you do not love yourself and soothe your soul and make sure you fill yourself up, the seeds of resentment will sprout and your relationships will falter. When you put yourself first, you commit to being the best you—your authentic self, your true self—so you can then be the best you for others—your family, your friends, your colleagues. Centering on self is an act of love.

Reflection

_____
_____
_____
_____
_____
_____
_____
_____
_____
_____
_____
_____
_____
_____
_____
_____
_____
_____
_____
_____
_____
_____
_____
_____
_____
_____
_____
_____
_____
_____
_____

Challenge

— ❖ ❖ ❖ —

CHALLENGE YOUR BODY. Challenge your mind. Challenge your soul. There are so many ways in which to challenge yourself for the better. However, many of you think of challenge as a negative, but that is not how it is intended to be. A challenge is not necessarily difficult, although sometimes it is and comes in the form of a lesson for the soul. A challenge can bring about positive change, positive thought, and positive action. It depends on how you view your life, whether you see the potential in a challenge or the strife. It is your choice how you view the challenges in your life.

First, let us talk about challenges of the body. Many have physical challenges to overcome in this life, and many have chosen to challenge their bodies to be stronger, faster, better, but for others it is just being able to overcome enough of their physical challenges so they can simply move, or walk, or do everyday chores and activities that some take for granted.

Challenges of the body are also affected by the mind, so let us talk about challenges of the mind. This is tricky, because as each and every one of you knows, the mind is the ego, and the ego wants to win every challenge, no matter the cost. So, the mind will create challenges sometimes where there are none.

All challenges of the mind, real or created, affect the spirit, the soul. It is in the challenge of the soul where you can heal and grow the most. It is in the challenge of the soul where the answers reside. The challenge of the soul is simply to achieve the lessons of a lifetime. To learn them, to be challenged by them, and to make the changes necessary to be true to your soul. The challenge of the soul is the challenge of the body, mind, and spirit working as one when all thoughts, feelings, words, actions, and reactions are in alignment. This is the challenge. It is the only challenge that matters in your life. Be in alignment.

Reflection

Change

❖ ❖ ❖

WHY ARE YOU so afraid of change? Why are you so afraid of the unknown? What you do not understand? Why is it so hard to leave your comfort zone, to step out into the unknown, to try and make a change that will help your soul, your fellow man, and the greater good? Why are you afraid of change?

Change is not something to be feared, nor is it something to be revered. It is simply part of living, part of growing, part of the evolution of the soul. Change is necessary, and you must ask yourself: What have I changed lately? What have I given up? What I have I started new? What have I changed in my daily rituals? Have I changed the way I speak? Have I changed the way I look at others, the way I treat others? Has this change been positive or negative?

Not all change is positive. Change should only be for the betterment of the soul and to help others. Simply put, change for the sake of change is not worthwhile. Change to run away from something or someone is not worthwhile. Change because you are bored and just want to try something different is not worthwhile. Change should always be looked upon in its purest, most honest form. Change in its honest form will always serve your soul. It will be for the betterment of your soul, and therefore the betterment of others.

Make the changes that are necessary for your soul, and make these changes now. What are you waiting for? Confirmation that you are making the right choice? Confirmation that the change will serve you?

If your intention is to grow and learn and improve your soul, then the change is necessary. If the decision to change is based in ego and is to run away from something or someone, then stop and ask yourself why. Why am I running away? Why am I seeking something or someone different? What is broken? What needs to heal? What needs to change within? What needs to change inside of me?

Always look within for the answers, and do not make a change just to get away, just to run from yourself. Because eventually the run will be over, the chase will end, and the change that you were running from will catch up with you. Make positive changes; make changes that are for your soul, not for the ego. Do not be afraid. Do not delay. Make the changes that are necessary today, and stop making changes that move you further away from your soul's purpose and ultimately your peace.

Reflection

Courage

❖ ❖ ❖

WHAT IS COURAGE? Is it the belief that you are invincible? The belief that you can do anything? The belief that nothing bad can happen? Or is it just the opposite? Is courage the belief that you are in fact not invincible, that you might be limited, and that you are threatened or in danger and going ahead anyway?

It is making the tough decisions, making the right choices, taking the first steps, moving forward instead of standing still. It is taking the risk, making the leap: that is courage. Courage is in the doing, not just the thinking. Courage is in the action; it is an act, not a thought. Anyone can think about doing something or saying something or believing something, but it takes courage to act on one's thoughts, to act on one's beliefs, to take on what might not work in one's favor.

Courage is doing it anyway because it is the right thing to do, not by society's standards, but your own. It is taking the first step, the first anything, into the truth of your own soul. It is speaking your truth, acting your truth, believing your truth. Not only does it take courage to take the first step, but sometimes it takes even more courage to continue, to continue the journey of healing, to continue the journey of self-awareness, to continue the journey inside yourself.

It takes courage to look deep within and accept what is there, even the parts that you have kept hidden from yourself. Let them come to light inside you and do not turn away. Look clearly at your shadows, not only to face them, but to allow them to be, to breathe, to live within you, and then, piece by piece, keep only what serves your soul and let the rest go. Letting go is an act of courage in and of itself, because letting go—whether of an old idea, thought, or belief, or even a person—it takes courage, and it takes initiative.

Again, courage is not thought, it is action. Courage is not strength of will, it is willingness to be strong. Courage is an act, an act of serving one's soul even in the face of everyone else's judgment or lack of understanding. Courage is authenticity in motion.

Reflection

Compassion

❖ ❖ ❖

WHAT IS COMPASSION? Is it feeling empathy for another human being? For mankind? For the planet? For yourself? It is all of the above. Having compassion is caring enough not only to feel something, but to do something. It is in the doing that one finds compassion. It is in the acting out and making a difference and being there for someone or for your loved ones, for the planet, or for yourself.

Compassion comes in many forms. It is the very essence of your soul, your spirit. A soul can soar, but only if there is compassion within. Ask yourself: Have I been compassionate today? Have I truly cared for another or for myself? Have I acted in ways that showed that I cared instead of just thinking about it?

You see, many can be compassionate sitting on the couch thinking about what they might do, but it is compassionate to get off the couch and actually be of service—be of service to mankind, be of service to the planet, be of service to yourself.

So, the very first and most important person to have compassion for is *you*. Yes, you. How can you learn compassion, how important it is, if you do not feel it first with the heart and soul? If you do not show yourself grace, how can you show another? If you do not care for yourself, how can you care for another? How can you care for the planet? How can you save humanity?

That is what we want: compassion for yourself, compassion for your loved ones, compassion for mankind, and compassion for the planet, in that order. Begin with yourself. Begin by giving yourself the compassion you need and deserve. Yes, you are worthy of compassion. Yes, you are worthy of love. Yes, you are worthy of the divine spark within you.

Reflection

_____
_____
_____
_____
_____
_____
_____
_____
_____
_____
_____
_____
_____
_____
_____
_____
_____
_____
_____
_____
_____
_____
_____
_____
_____
_____
_____
_____
_____
_____

Compassion for Self

❖ ❖ ❖

COMPASSION COMES IN all forms, all shapes and sizes, and has no price tag or expiration date. Compassion is the backbone of love, as it lifts you up and carries you and those around you through some of the darker times in life. Do not forget that you are human, that you will make mistakes, and that someone has shown you compassion at one time or another.

It is compassion that leads the way to forgiveness. It is compassion that leads the way to acceptance, and it is compassion that will lead the way to love—love of yourself, most importantly. How, you may ask, can I show compassion to myself? I know how to be compassionate with others around me, but how do I know I am being compassionate with myself? It is actually very simple. Any words you say to yourself, any actions you take that directly affect you, any reactions you have that are or are not in alignment with your truth are opportunities for compassion.

Would you have compassion for someone with physical flaws? Would you have compassion for someone who mentally is not as intelligent or knowledgeable? Would you have compassion for someone who has lost his or her way and seems to be surrounded by darkness, unable to find his or her own light? If the answer is yes, then you are capable of being compassionate for others, and therefore for yourself.

Show compassion to that part of you that dislikes your physical form, show compassion for that part of you that questions your own judgments or decisions, show compassion for that part of you that sometimes, despite what you know, does the very thing that hurts you the most. Show compassion for your own heart, and then you can show compassion for others through your own experiences, your own truths, your own mistakes. Show compassion. Be compassion. Allow compassion into your life.

Elizabeth Pelkey

Reflection

Creativity

❖ ❖ ❖

CREATIVITY OF THE mind, creativity of the soul, creativity of the universe. Each of you has within the creativity of your own soul. Creativity is simply to create, and each of you has the ability to create your own reality, to create that which serves your soul, and that which will serve others.

Do not let the trials of everyday life stifle your creative voice, your creative spirit, and your creative talent within. Do not let the worry of being accepted stifle your creative voice, your creative vision, and your creative soul. Do not let the worries of the mundane stifle your creative spirit, your creative drive, and your creative determination. Do not let trivial matters that are not relevant to the big picture cloud your creativity. Do not let the wonder leave your spirit. Do not let the desire to be unique leave your soul.

Be creative in all that you do, in all that you say, in all that you are. Each of you has talents beyond your own imagination. Some of you write, some of you paint, some of you dance, some of you speak words of truth, some of you share experiences with others, some of you teach, some of you heal, and all of you love. Let your creative self run free, and do not be stifled by your own insecurities, by your own feelings of inadequacy, as you are creative beyond measure and are only limited by your own disbelief.

Believe in your innate ability to create. To create a life, to create relationships, to create a path, to create a journey, to create a future for yourself that serves you and your soul. For whatever serves your soul will also serve the greater good. Create that which will serve your soul and, in turn, serve the greater good.

Challenge yourself to create a life that is a monument to your own spirit. That is true to who *you* are and not what someone else's idea of you may be. Be creative, be free, be love, be you. Create your dreams and make them your reality. Create so that others can see your shining example, and then they will also create that which is unique to their life, to their soul, and then to the greater good. See, just one of you creating will create another and will create another and will create another, and so on and so on and so on. Creativity. It is the continuation of the being, the life, the soul, the universe.

Reflection

Doubt

——— ❖ ❖ ❖ ———

Why do you doubt? Why do you doubt yourself, your abilities, your lovers, your friends, your family, your job, your circumstances? Doubt binds you to the ego. Doubt binds your soul and does not let you live on your soul's path. Doubt is an insidious creature feeding on your self-esteem, your self-worth, and your soul. Doubt comes strictly from ego. It comes from fear—be it fear of failure or even fear of success.

Think about what it is that you doubt. Do you doubt yourself, or are you really doubting those around you? Those who tell you are wrong or those who judge you or make you feel like you are less than. Is the doubt coming from within you or from outside of you? It is important to note the difference, as doubt that comes from around you and outside of you can easily be silenced. However, the doubt that comes from within is much more difficult to let go of—difficult, but not impossible.

First, you need to look deeply into this negative emotion called doubt. You must feel it; you must breathe it in, sit with it, and then go about dissecting it. Ask yourself these three questions: What am I doubting? Who am I doubting? What or who is making me doubt? Do I doubt myself, or is this a reflection of the doubt I see in others? Do I really doubt myself or my abilities, or am I just afraid of the outcome? Am I afraid to try, and to possibly fail or possibly succeed, or both?

If your doubt is a reflection of someone else, look away. Just as you would turn away from a mirror, look away from the doubt in others' eyes. That is their fear shining through them and has nothing to do with you. Doubt from within—this is something to overcome. The ego is strong within all of you. It is who you are in this incarnation. Ego is strong and does not like to give in so easily to the spirit and the soul. It wants to keep control.

When you set out on your soul's path and try something new and different, your ego is uncomfortable with this and may try to sabotage your decision by filling your mind with doubt. When this happens, logic is more useful than emotion. The emotion centered around doubt is fear, so if you can detach from this feeling, you can look at it in a different way. Doubt is only your ego's way of saying no. Ego does not like change, as change is uncomfortable. To your soul, change is necessary, change is life, change is beautiful, and change is beyond doubt. It is faith. It is believing. It is understanding. It is awareness of your path. Let go of doubt, let go of fear, let go and begin to change.

Reflection

Expansion

❖ ❖ ❖

EXPANSION OF THE mind. Expansion of the heart. Expansion of the soul. In all the ways that humans can expand in a lifetime, it is the expansion of one's soul that will lead one to peace. However, in order to reach the soul, one must expand one's mind and be open to new possibilities, new realities, new existence.

In order to expand one's heart, one must expand one's compassion, one's kindness, one's intent, so that all words, actions, and reactions come from a place of love that resides in the heart. The more love that is given, the more love that is received. The more open a heart is to receive, the more that heart can give, so once the mind is expanded, then the heart expands, until one day there is the soul. Waiting, as always, for the human to wake up and notice, notice that there is more to living than just existing, that there is more joy to be found than sorrow, that there is so much *more* to life.

This is the soul's expansion, the soul's awakening, and the entryway to the divine within. It has always been there, but it is in the awakening and then the understanding that the soul can expand, and expand to its capacity, in a lifetime, which is infinite. There are infinite possibilities once the soul expands, so expand your mind to include new ways of thinking, expand your heart to see news ways of loving, and then allow your soul to expand to new ways of loving yourself, loving others, loving humanity, loving the earth.

Expansion is necessary to life—not only yours, but the lives of those around you. Expansion is necessary for peace. Expansion is necessary to life on Earth.

Reflection

_____

_____

_____

_____

_____

_____

_____

_____

_____

_____

_____

_____

_____

_____

_____

_____

_____

_____

_____

_____

_____

_____

_____

_____

_____

_____

Family

$\diamond \quad \diamond \quad \diamond$

FIRST AND FOREMOST, whatever your belief system, your soul chose your parents, and if you have children, your children chose you. This fact immediately allows you to separate yourself from the ego's fear-based thoughts and feelings that arise regarding family. It can explain so much about why you feel close to some members of your family but not others. It explains and can help you to understand that you have soul contracts with all of your family members, some stronger or more important than others.

Your soul chose your parents—even if you were not given the love you wanted or needed. This does not mean you are paying for some wrong you have done in this life, or even another life. It is not karma. It is your soul wanting to learn a lesson to understand all sides of life on Earth, of being human, of making mistakes, of not being loved the way you wish. You are loved, even if you were loved too much or not enough.

Family can be your greatest source of joy and your greatest source of pain. You can work through pain the more you understand its origin. If you asked for this lifetime to be one of betrayal and learning how to overcome and trust, for example, you might be betrayed first by those you are supposed to trust the most. Some of you are reading this and thinking, "I have the best parents in the world," and maybe you think so, but your sibling might not feel the same way. You all come in with different lessons, therefore different expectations for what constitutes a happy family.

When you are triggered by the past in the present, recognize it as an opportunity for understanding. Many times, you will fall in love with or even marry someone exactly like your mother or your father, and at some point you will become aware that negative emotions are coming to the surface in your present relationship that are simply too strong or just don't fit the current situation. This is your clue that the negative emotion is from the past. Allow the negative emotion to come up, and attach it to a memory of the past that more than likely will follow. This will give you an opportunity to not only begin to heal the past but separate it from your present relationship.

Awareness and intent will be your friends as you navigate the lessons of your childhood. And just as you were affected by your parents, remember that your children chose you with all your imperfections to be or not to be the kind of parent they want or need in order to learn the lessons of their lifetime.

Reflection

Fear

WHY MUST YOU fear one another? Why is everyone afraid? Fear comes from within, not from what is outside of you. Fear of another is a wasted emotion and will never serve your soul.

Fear is the one emotion that creates other negative emotions: Jealousy comes from the fear of not living up to another's expectations, anger comes from the fear that something will be or has been taken from you, lust comes from the fear that you are not lovable, despair comes from the fear that nothing will ever be different or that nothing will ever change, temptation comes from the fear that what one has is not good enough, greed comes from the fear of losing or not having enough.

We could keep going, but our hope is that you now understand that fear is a master that will always control you. You will never and can never control fear. Fear controls you. Don't you see? You fear losing control, but the very act of being afraid controls you. Any decision, and we mean *any* decision, that is made from a place of fear will not serve you, and it will not serve your soul. It will only lead you away from peace, away from love, away from not only your own good, but the good of the world. Look at your fear. Face your fear. Let go of your fear. You will see that fear, and once you let it go, it will never control you again.

Reflection

Feelings

———— ❖ ❖ ❖ ————

FEELINGS OF LOVE, feelings of desire, feelings of rage, feelings of pain, feelings of hope, feelings of hate. Notice your feelings. Are they dark or are they light? Do they serve you? Do they serve your soul? Or do they create darkness within?

You are the keeper of your own feelings, which means that you and only you can control how you feel. As you know by now, you cannot control the world or the people around you, but you can control how you feel and how you react. It is not always possible to shield yourself from negative energy, negative people, and negative events; however, you can do this as much as humanly possible in your day-to-day life.

Avoid the news, avoid opening web links to articles about death and destruction, avoid television shows that depict graphic violent images or promote meanness and gossip, avoid people in your life who seem to carry with them a cloud of negativity and darkness. Avoid the darkness you can control. Do this, and then you can address the negativity within, which will in turn help you feel the light and not the darkness.

When the unavoidable negative actions or negative words or negative energy arises, first allow yourself to feel the emotions that rise up, and then let them go. Usually you feel first what emotion has been constricting you in your daily life, and this is the reason you get angry at an event that has nothing to do with you. Your anger is yours and yours alone, and any negative event will bring up any darkness that is within. Let it out, acknowledge it, and let it go. Let it out, acknowledge it, and let it go.

Remember, any negative feelings you harbor within you will come out whenever any negativity is around you. Avoid all that you can, protect yourself with a shield of light energy. Set the intention that you will release all negative emotion and will only carry with you that which is light.

Light is *lighter*. Can you not tell how heavy and pulled down you feel when carrying negative feelings inside of you? Release all that is negative within you, including negative feelings about your own actions, your own body, and your own soul. Release and you will automatically feel lighter. Once you release the negative feelings within yourself, you will find that uncontrollable negative events in the world no longer have any power over you. Your feelings will be yours and yours alone.

Reflection

_____

_____

_____

_____

_____

_____

_____

_____

_____

_____

_____

_____

_____

_____

_____

_____

_____

_____

_____

_____

_____

_____

_____

_____

_____

_____

_____

_____

_____

_____

_____

Forgiveness

———— ❖ ❖ ❖ ————

FORGIVENESS OF OTHERS. Forgiveness of self. Forgiveness—what is it, exactly? All hear the words forgive and you shall be set free, forgive and you shall find peace, forgive because it is you and not the other person you are forgiving. But what exactly is forgiveness, and how does one forgive?

Forgiveness is allowing what happened in the past to stay in the past and not affect your present. Forgiveness is not allowing the past to haunt you, to make you sad or angry or fearful. Forgiveness is realizing that no matter what you could have or should have or would have done, it cannot be changed and never will be changed. What needs to be forgiven simply cannot be taken away; it cannot leave your consciousness, as it is part of what makes up who you are. However, it does not have to guide you; it does not have to lead you to the negative and to the darkness.

This is why is it is imperative that you forgive those who have hurt you in the past. To forgive is to accept that nothing can be changed, that nothing can be different, and to hold onto feelings of hate, powerlessness, loss will only destroy what you are searching for in your present and want for your future: peace.

How to forgive is complicated, and different for each individual. For some of you, forgiveness seemingly comes easily, the words slip off your tongue. But do you truly believe what you are saying? Are you truly forgiving the wrongs of your past? This is the key—you must believe in the forgiveness you are giving. You must believe in your heart and soul that this person, this event, this situation, is forgivable and that you can let go of the hope that it could have been different, that it could have not happened, and then you let go. You let go of the pain of the past and you forgive. To forgive is to heal.

Reflection

Forgiveness of Self

BUT WHAT ABOUT forgiveness of self? This forgiveness is the most important of all, because without self-forgiveness, peace cannot be found. Forgiveness of self does not come as easily, because in order to forgive yourself, you have to face all of your own wrongdoings, all of your own words and actions that hurt others, no matter the reason. You have to face the demons within and make peace with yourself.

Forgive yourself with the understanding that you are no longer that person, that you are now aware of your own words and actions and can release them. Forgiveness of self is acknowledging your own shortcomings, your own weaknesses, and coming to terms with the mistakes of the past. They cannot be undone, therefore why not forgive? You cannot take back any unkind words or actions, but you can atone for them. You can learn from them. You can grow from them. You can begin to understand just why you did what you need to forgive. Understanding will lead to forgiveness, and forgiveness will lead you to peace.

Remember that to forgive is to heal, and to forgive yourself will bring about the most healing. This is how important forgiveness is to your own self-worth, to your own happiness, and to your own inner peace.

Elizabeth Pelkey

Reflection

Freedom

WHAT DOES FREEDOM mean to you? What does the word actually mean to you? Is it being free from someone or something? Is it freedom from want? Freedom from need? Freedom from your job, your responsibilities, your children, your parents, your friends, your own self? What does it mean to you?

How much are you willing to do to obtain the true freedom? The freedom of the soul. The freedom of inner peace, the freedom of a soaring spirit, the freedom of a soul at peace, the freedom of a heart and soul that are working together for not only your good, but the greater good. This is what freedom really is—everything else is just an illusion.

Find the freedom in and of your own soul. Walk the path—your path—and you will be free. Heal your pain, your past, and you will feel free. Let go of the burdens and the shackles that bind you to the past, and you will be free. Let go, and you will be free. Let go, and you will be set free.

Do you not see that it is not freedom from the material earthly world that will bring you peace? It is freedom from your own pain and fear, and this freedom comes with a price—a price many are not willing to pay. It takes work, a lot of hard work. It takes going inside to see what is really going on inside of you. It is looking very closely at your past—not just at what happened *to* you, but also what happened *because* of you.

It is laying bare the wounds of the past so they can heal. It is awareness, it is acceptance, and it is forgiveness. It is letting go of all the negative emotion that has been held down in order to protect you from feeling the pain. Only in release of this past emotion can you move forward. Only the forgiveness of others and, most important, yourself will bring the ultimate freedom. Freedom of the spirit. Freedom of the soul. Freedom from the pain and suffering of the past.

Free yourself from the past. Free yourself from all that is weighing you down, keeping you down, and not letting you fully live in the present: your own fear. Your own fear of looking too deep, of acknowledging too much, of *feeling* the negative emotions. Fear will always, always keep you from being free. Find the fear within and let it go. Do the work necessary to heal, and you will be free. Are you willing to pay the price for your own freedom?

Reflection

Greed

❖ ❖ ❖

WHY IS EVERYONE on Earth so preoccupied with greed, with money? How much does one person need? Greed will be the death of society if it is not brought under control. The 1 percent, ha! Their souls, for the most part—there are a few good souls out there—are in their infancy and will have to pay a penance in the next lifetime. Stealing from people to get ahead? That is not what was intended when the stock market came to fruition.

We are worried, dear one, about your society, and we are afraid that the worst is yet to come. You and others like you who let go of personal possessions are on the right path; you have it right. Why hold onto possessions that no longer serve you or, more important, aren't needed at all? Why purchase something just so others can see it and get jealous, be envious?

Envy, jealousy, and greed all stem from one emotion: fear. Fear of losing, fear of winning, fear of the past, fear of the future, fear of the self, fear of others. The entire world lives in fear. Fear is your enemy. Fear is unnecessary. It breeds discontent, and it breeds restlessness, and it breeds distrust.

Many souls ask, how do we let go of fear? That is part of the healing process, to let go of old habits and memories that are holding you trapped in fear. Any decision made from a place of fear will not serve your soul in the long run. Your soul needs to be free from the past and open to the present. Fear is your enemy, plain and simple. Is this not simple enough for others to understand?

We know it is necessary to speak the same language of the populace and not sound as high and mighty as those who let greed rule their life. Let go of the money, let go of the possessions, let go of the greed, let go of the fear. Heal. Once your soul has healed and you are at peace with the world, you will see that you need very little to live a fulfilling and peaceful life. Let go.

Elizabeth Pelkey

Reflection

Hope. Salvation. Faith.

❖ ❖ ❖

THERE IS HOPE in humanity. There is always hope, and with this hope will come salvation for all, for every human who walks the earth regardless of their faith. Do you not see that any faith is true? That any faith is real? That any faith is to be believed and respected? To hope and to have faith is to have salvation, and this is not just for Christians, or Jews, or Hindus, or Buddhists, or Muslims. This is for every single human on the planet.

Move beyond the differences between religions. Move beyond the differences of your faith and look for the similarities. Do you not see that love is love? That prayer is prayer? That healing is healing? That kindness is kindness? That belief is belief? That life everlasting is life everlasting? Find the similarities and open your arms to your fellow man. It is our hope and it is the key to your salvation and to the earth's salvation that you have faith in each other. Believe whatever you want to believe, as long as it is for the greater good, as long as it is for the greater good of humanity.

Don't you see that by excluding yourself, by thinking you are the only chosen people, you are going against the very principles you follow? It is the same for those of you who only have faith in your own abilities, your own intellect, and your own world. You do not have to believe in a higher power to be kind to others, to help humanity, and to do good in the world. Hope, salvation, and faith come in many different shapes and sizes, in many different forms, and one is not better than any other. In fact, you are more similar that you are different.

Look beyond the differences, look beyond what is on the surface, and look within the hearts and souls of your fellow humans. This is what is the same, this is what is important, and this is what needs to be saved: human beings caring, loving, and respecting one another. This is our hope, this is your salvation, and this is faith. Faith in mankind.

Reflection

Hunger

❖ ❖ ❖

WHAT IS IT that you hunger for? Is it knowledge? Is it love? Is it lust? Is it forgiveness? You must feed your soul, as no other person will be able to satiate the hunger of your soul. It is a hunger that comes from a longing deep inside you. If you are hungry for something, anything, then it is something that is lacking in your life. Do not fill up on what does not nourish the soul.

Many eat to fulfill another kind of hunger, another need; many spend to fulfill another kind of hunger, another need; and many drink or take drugs to fulfill yet another kind of hunger, another need. Many hurt themselves and others because their soul is hungry. You can feed your soul through growth and healing.

You can feed your soul by surrounding yourself with positivity. You can feed your soul by finding your own singular path, the path to your inner peace. But it must begin with you. You cannot look to another to "feed" you, because you will not be satisfied. Initially, you will think that you are, but you will soon find that the hunger returns. Your soul must be kept fed. Feed your soul.

Only you can know the inner peace that comes from knowing your own soul, from healing your own soul, from gently loving your own soul. Only you. Love yourself enough to feed *yourself* what *you* need to grow and learn in order to be happy and find peace. Surround yourself with love, the divine love that is within each and every one of you. You do not need "things" to feel satisfied or whole. You need only the divine light within your soul. When hungry, look within. Nourishment comes from within. Always from within. Feed your soul, nourish your light, and love and peace will find you.

Reflection

Intelligence

— ❖ ❖ ❖ —

WHAT IS IT, really? Is it knowledge learned simply for the sake of knowing something so one can feel superior to someone else? This is not intelligence, this is superiority. Is it learning if one wants to forget something from the past, or rather to change the past through knowledge? This is not intelligence, this is regret. Intelligence is enriching the mind, which in turn enriches the soul.

One must seek knowledge. Seek and you shall find the knowledge you need to grow your soul and learn the lessons of this lifetime. The greatest intelligence of all is to seek what one is lacking, what one is afraid of, and what one is least likely to find. The harder the search, the more important the find. Intelligence is not just being smarter than someone else, it is knowing that you and someone else are more alike than not. That you and another person may be on a similar path, a similar journey, with similar obstacles. One learns, while the other does not notice the lessons before him.

Which one are you? Do your lessons pass you by like a train leaving the station? Are you too busy to notice that a lesson has come and gone? That an opportunity for growth—for soul intelligence—has been lost? It is never too late to learn the lessons one must learn to find peace in this lifetime, but one must be open, one must seek out truth, one must look beyond the obvious, and one must not ignore the message.

This knowledge may not be what one wants to know or experience, but if it is necessary for soul growth, then it must be accepted and learned. Without this knowledge, this intelligence, one will live a life of ignorance.

Choose to learn, to be aware, to grow, and to change. Being willing to change and learn from one's lessons is true intelligence. This intelligence will not make you superior, but it will make you know yourself and know your soul. You will then believe in the power of knowledge and the peace that comes from within.

Reflection

Journey

❖ ❖ ❖

JOURNEY TO THE path of your soul. A journey of a thousand steps begins with just one. Do you not see? Why, then, are so many afraid to take this journey inward, into the soul, into the depths of the soul? It is necessary to journey back, to journey back to past trauma, and it is necessary to journey into darkness in order to find the light. It is necessary to take this long and sometimes never-ending journey to healing. You must walk the path that is put in front of you. For some, the path is hiding behind self-deception or the longing for a life that is not yours to have.

You must be willing to follow your path wherever it leads you, no matter how frightening, no matter how treacherous, no matter how insurmountable it may seem. This is a journey of the soul, for the soul, and no one can walk this path with you. No one can feel what you feel, and no one else can take away the pain. Only your own journey inward will heal the pain that is inside of you. In order to heal, you must take this journey back to the origin of the pain, the anger, the shame, and ultimately the fear. It is fear that is holding you back, fear that is keeping you from taking this journey; it is fear of the unknown, or fear of what you know awaits you there.

You have been given the strength that is necessary for the journey your soul has chosen. Do not forget that you are given all the strength you need for whatever your soul's journey might be. You have been given the gifts that will assist you along your path, and more will be revealed the farther along the path you go. Go down this path, follow your soul, heal your past, and find the journey home.

It is, you know, a journey home—a journey home to yourself, to the inner peace you want so badly but are so afraid to find. Fear is holding you back. Do not let the fear of the past hold you back from the present and from your future—your soul's future. It is this future that is bright, it is this future that is at peace, is it this future at the end of this seemingly endless journey of your soul where you will find peace. Take this journey, follow your path, let go of the fear, and find your peace. It is right there waiting for you.

Elizabeth Pelkey

Reflection

Joy

❖ ❖ ❖

ONE HAS TO experience life to experience joy, one has to experience
selflessness to experience joy, one has to experience kindness to feel
joy, and one has to desire what is best for others to find joy. Joy is
always out there, just out there, waiting to be found. Joy is always,
always there, but sometimes you make decisions that send you in
the opposite direction of joy, in the opposite direction of your soul's
journey, away from who you really are and further and further away
from joy.

Are you one of those souls who is always wandering, always wonder-
ing, always waiting for joy to come to you, when in fact you must find
joy within? It is already inside you, waiting to be felt, to be experienced
and shared and delighted in and, most important, experienced through
the heart and inevitably through the soul. Go and find your joy within.
Heal the wounds of the past, forgive who you need to forgive, let go of
what haunts you, heal what is inside of you that makes you run from the
very joy you seek.

Joy is available to every soul, no matter what age, gender, race, class,
or creed—joy is universal. Feel joy this season and find this joy within.
Go inside your own heart and soul and find what may be lost, as it is
not lost forever. It is inside you just waiting to be found. Joy. Joy. Joy.
The word is so simple yet so complex, so short yet so long in memory,
so beautiful yet so often not expressed.

Joy can be experienced in moments, minutes, hours, days, weeks, or years, but they are all equally powerful. Remember that even one seemingly tiny moment of joy lives long in the mind and even longer in the soul. Find your joy. Feel your joy. Share your joy. Joy is a gift. Give and you shall receive.

Reflection

_____
_____
_____
_____
_____
_____
_____
_____
_____
_____
_____
_____
_____
_____
_____
_____
_____
_____
_____
_____
_____
_____
_____
_____
_____
_____
_____
_____
_____

Justice

————— ❖ ❖ ❖ —————

THERE IS so much talk about justice, but what makes there a reason for justice? What is going on that makes justice a necessity? Why are human beings not treating one another with the respect they deserve? A world without the need for justice is a world that is at peace. A world where there is no need for retribution is a world that is at peace, but it begins with the child, it begins at the beginning. Don't you see that it all starts at the beginning?

You come into this world with no prejudice, with no animosity, with no hate, with no fear, with no bitterness, with no need for justice. Then why, oh why do you grow up and become the one who uses, the one who abuses, the one who goes astray, the one who hates, the one who belittles, the one who is angry, the one who is fearful, the one who needs justice, or the one who takes it away? Why? What has happened to you when you cannot love your fellow man, when you cannot find it in your heart and soul to love, to cherish, to treat others with respect and dignity? All people, all your brothers and sisters, all souls.

Don't you realize that you are all one? That in your soul there are absolutely no differences of race, sexuality, gender, class, situation? You are all the same. Wake up! Wake up! Wake up and realize that each and every one of you has a part to play and has to shoulder some of the blame. Maybe you are someone who claims to not be biased, not be prejudiced, not be above anyone else. Look inside: is this really true? Is this really how you behave on a minute-by-minute basis?

It is human to have negative thoughts, to look down upon someone when you yourself look down upon yourself. It all comes back to loving yourself. If you do not love yourself, if you do not respect yourself, how can you expect to ever love or respect anyone else? There will always be someone or something that bears the brunt of your discomfort with your own soul. This is why it is imperative that you heal your wounds, that you heal your pain, that you heal your soul. If each and every individual on Earth would heal, then there would never be a reason for justice to be served.

Elizabeth Pelkey

Reflection

Justification

❖ ❖ ❖

WHY IS IT that souls on Earth feel the need to justify their every thought, every word, every action? This need to justify comes directly from the ego self, as this is where doubt, need for acceptance, and fear reside. Fear of not being understood, fear of not doing what one should, fear of not being accepted.

Justification is contrary to what the soul needs. The need for justification is not in alignment with the soul. When you walk in your soul's path, there is no need for justification, there is no need for approval, there is no need for questioning of any kind. You will simply know, and you will simply feel it to be right and true. You will never have to justify your thoughts, words, or actions to anyone or anything at any time.

Does this not sound better than going through your life looking for acceptance, seeking acceptance, where many times there is none to be found? Does this not sound better than constantly feeling as though someone else has to agree with you or do things the way you do? Then stop looking for justification. Follow your soul's path and you will not have to question, you will not have to ask, you will not need to seek the approval of others, and you will never have to justify your thoughts, words, or actions again.

When you are walking your soul's path, when you find the inner peace you have been searching for, you will make decisions in this heart-centered space and every thought, word, and action will be justified by simply being, by simply existing, by simply coming from a place of love and acceptance and peace. No justification will ever be needed.

So, why do you wait? Why do you wait? Why do you wait to walk your soul's path? For so many of you, this path is visible, if only out of the corner of your eye. You know this to be true, you know this to be right for you, and some part of you wants this so desperately, but you are afraid. You are afraid, and it is time to find the courage within, the courage to speak your truth, to live your truth, to be a shining example of living in your soul's path and never seeking justification again. Your thoughts, words, and actions will be as pure as your soul. You will think, speak, and act from a place of love and light. Love and light do not need approval. Love and light do not need acceptance. Love and light do not need justification.

Reflection

_____
_____
_____
_____
_____
_____
_____
_____
_____
_____
_____
_____
_____
_____
_____
_____
_____
_____
_____
_____
_____
_____
_____
_____
_____
_____
_____
_____
_____
_____

Love

‒ ❖ ❖ ❖ ‒

SUCH A SIMPLE word, but oh so powerful. Love is what is within each and every one of you. Love is the greatest healer. Love is divine, and the divine is love. Each and every one of you has divine love within *you*. This love sometimes is hidden or undiscovered, because if you are not healed, this divine love cannot come from within you.

It is of the utmost importance that this divine love is shared on Earth. Heal what is broken. Heal what is in the past. Heal what has been taken from your spirit. Heal so that the divine love within all can be unleashed. Do you not know the power that comes from such a divine source? Do you not know the power that comes from love? Love in its purest divine form? From love that is all-encompassing and all-healing?

It is the necessary force that will heal the Earth. Pure love. Pure divine love will heal the Earth. But first you need to heal the hurt inside of you, so that your divine love can shine through and you can be one with pure love. Be one with the divine. Be one with love. Love: four letters that are the greatest force in the universe. Love.

Self-love, love of self, is sometimes the hardest love of all. It doesn't seem to be true at first glance, but it is the one goal of every soul to get to the place in a lifetime where one can love oneself, where one can find true acceptance, true forgiveness, true and full worthiness. Now, it may not be easy but it is possible. In order to love oneself, one must be centered on the self and on the healing and growth necessary in a lifetime. Love of self is *not* selfish, it is simply loving oneself enough to say no in order to say yes, to leave in order to stay true to one's soul, to walk away in order to walk toward self. Self-love is personal, singular, and without walls. Self-love cannot wear a mask, nor does it need to. It is seeing the beauty of one's soul.

Elizabeth Pelkey

Reflection

Lomalty

— ❖ ❖ ❖ —

To WHOM ARE you loyal? If being loyal is being true or in your truth to another, then being loyal is actually being yourself and trusting someone else to be authentic back to you. If not, why are you loyal? It is sometimes said that loyalty comes at a price, that sometimes a soul can be loyal to those who hurt it or have hurt it in the past and it's still loyal. Is this being loyal to a fault? Is there fault in loyalty?

Think about who is currently loyal to you, and think about those you are loyal to. Do they match? Does the loyalty you give find its way back to you? This is not always the case so carefully choose who you are loyal to, who deserves your loyalty. Who do you want to be loyal to in this life? It is your choice. It is always your choice, and by same notion, just because someone is loyal to you, do you owe it back to that person? What if his or her loyalty comes with a price? What if his or her loyalty means you cannot be your true authentic self around that person? Is loyalty worth it if it does not come hand-in-hand with truth and authenticity?

It is time to take stock of your life and those you allow in it. Yes, those you allow in your life. You have a choice, even if it means finding other employment or retreating from a friendship that has become harmful. Choose who you wish to remain loyal to in this life. First and foremost, are you loyal to yourself? Do you show yourself the same courtesy and the same trust that you give others? If not, ask yourself why. Am I being my authentic self and being true to myself? Am I being faithful to who I am inside? Loyalty. Fidelity. Faithfulness. They all begin with you.

Reflection

Meditation versus Contemplation

❖ ❖ ❖

WHAT IS THE difference, you ask? The difference lies in the intent. To contemplate is to think, to use your brain, to think of the past, of the old patterns that have followed you throughout your life. To meditate is to not think, to not allow words of consciousness, to allow all words all thoughts to leave the station, so to speak, so that you can actually hear the words of the highest self, of the guides and angels.

So you see, contemplation comes from the mind and meditation comes from the heart. If the mind is ego and is fear-based, and the heart is the soul and is love-based, it becomes simply the difference between thinking about something from a place of fear and uncertainty or meditating and allowing your divine light, your highest self, to emerge and speak from your soul. The words may come, but they will feel different. They will not scare you. They will not necessarily give you what you want either. It is the ability to quiet the mind so one can listen to the soul.

Practice quieting your mind enough to hear your own soul. How do you do this? Certainly you have read much about how to meditate, but is there anything that tells you how to not contemplate? To contemplate is to think about the past or the future. Rarely is it about the present. But meditation is all about the here and now. Take the time to be present—in your surroundings, in your body, yes, in your mind, and then in your soul. Set the intention that you wish to meditate with love from a heart-centered space, and allow contemplation with fear from an ego-centered space to leave. Be in the present, the present being the exact moment you are meditating. If you are thinking about earlier in the day, that is not the present, it is the past. If you are thinking about what will be after you meditate, that is the future. The present is now. It is the moment of meditation. Set your intention to meditate in the here and now. Allow your guides and angels to guide you. Allow yourself to be one in the moment, mind, body, and soul.

Elizabeth Pelkey

Reflection

Memories

❖ ❖ ❖

MEMORIES OF YESTERDAY. Memories of the past. Memories that haunt your mind and your soul. What do you do with these memories of old? Do you put them away in a box, hoping you will never have to open them? Do you pretend they never happened? Do you hide them away, hoping they will never be found?

No matter what you try to do, memories will always come to the surface, and usually when least expected. Memories of the past are like sand—they slip through your fingers but remain embedded somehow in the skin. Tiny bits of sand remain just underneath the skin, and they will begin to bother you, they will begin to annoy you, they will scratch at you wanting to get out, wanting to be remembered, wanting to be felt.

Don't you see that memories of the past—those memories that are painful, that haunt you, that were too great for you to feel at the time—will come out? They will come out. They will come out, so why not address them head-on? Why not choose to feel the memories of your past so that you can heal? Why not do it before the feelings of those memories come out and sabotage your life in ways that can damage your present happiness?

Choose to face your memories. Choose to face your decisions. Choose to face your doubts and your shame and your anger and your fear. Choose to allow these memories to come out, to be felt, and then to fade away. Only then will you find peace, only then will you feel whole, only then will you be fully released from the past. Believe it or not, it is the memories of goodness, the memories of kindness, the positive memories that sustained you through the worst of times that can help to release those memories you cannot face. It is the good, it is the light, and it is the memory of the pleasant and the pure and the clear that will aid you. So, bring up all the memories you have—both the dark and the light—and let the light help you to release the dark. Let your light release you from the darkness. Let your light bring you the peace you have been searching for. Remember, remember, remember, and let the light outshine the darkness.

Reflection

_____
_____
_____
_____
_____
_____
_____
_____
_____
_____
_____
_____
_____
_____
_____
_____
_____
_____
_____
_____
_____
_____
_____
_____
_____
_____
_____
_____
_____
_____

Necessity

❖ ❖ ❖

WHAT IS ABSOLUTELY necessary in your life? What do you feel you could not do without? Is it love? Is it money? Is it friendship? Is it marriage or a partnership of some kind? Is it children? Is it freedom? Is it being heard? Is it being seen and felt? Is it to be at peace? Take a look at your life and decide what is actually necessary. But necessary for what? For your happiness? For your contentment? For your pride? For your soul? What is really necessary for your soul?

This is what you must ask yourself—what is necessary for your soul. Not someone else's, not society's, but your own soul. What is necessary in life to bring you the peace you seek? What is necessary in your life to feed your soul? Take stock of your life and look at what is *not* necessary. In fact, look at what is doing just the opposite of feeding your soul— look at what is taking from your own peace of mind. Make the changes necessary. Make the sometimes difficult choices that you know deep in your heart will serve your soul.

There is only so much that is truly necessary: love, kindness, cooperation, respect, trust, and peace. Clean out the closets of your life, both literally and metaphorically. Give away that which no longer serves you. Give away that which brings you any negative emotion. Give away that which does not guide you to your highest self. Give away. Give away. Give away. Do not hold onto "things" from the past that only serve as reminders of what could have been or what was so very painful.

Why are you holding on? Why are you keeping that which does not serve your soul? What is your attachment? Is it a healthy attachment? Is it a necessity? Ask yourself why. Why do I keep that which is only a reminder of what I, in fact, do not want to be reminded of and no longer need in my life? Give away and let go. It is time to give away and let go. Keep only that which is necessary to your peace, to your happiness, to your well-being. Only that which brings love, kindness, cooperation, respect, trust, and peace. This is what is necessary. Nothing more and nothing less.

Elizabeth Pelkey

Reflection

Pain

❖ ❖ ❖

THE PAIN YOU feel inside. The pain you feel in your body. The pain you feel in your mind. The pain you feel in your soul. Are they connected? Of course they are. All hurt and pain are intertwined, as the body, mind, and soul are intertwined. They must all three be in harmony in order for the hurt to diminish and eventually go away.

Some carry wounds of the past like shields of protection from present or future hurt, but this will not last, as it will only cause more damage to the soul. Hurt and pain are only felt on the earthly plane, and therefore can be transcended through healing. Get to the root of your pain, get to the source of your pain, and get to the memory of your pain. Everyone experiences hurt and pain in their lifetime, and each and every one of you is carrying this hurt with you right now. It is human nature. It is part of being, and it is part of living.

In order to be at peace, however, one must learn to lower the layers of protection, acknowledge the pain of the past, accept that it happened, forgive those who need to be forgiven, and release the pain. Release all the negative emotions attached to the hurt and pain: grief, doubt, shame, anger, self-hatred, and fear. Release the pain of the past, and it will no longer affect your present. Release all the hurt inside of your soul, and your body and mind will heal and be whole again. Your body will thrive, your mind will be clear, and your soul will sing.

Hurt. It is human nature to hurt and be hurt by others. It is human nature to protect oneself from hurt by keeping it buried inside and not dealing with the negative emotions as they arise. Please remember that this is not protection, and this is not healing. You can only heal by acknowledging, by accepting, by forgiving, and by letting go. Let go of all your pain. Reclaim your body, your mind, and your soul. Be free from pain and hurt, and heal. It is time. It is time. It is time.

Reflection

_____

_____

_____

_____

_____

_____

_____

_____

_____

_____

_____

_____

_____

_____

_____

_____

_____

_____

_____

_____

_____

_____

_____

_____

_____

_____

_____

_____

_____

Peace

❖ ❖ ❖

PEACE IS THE prize. It is what all souls are striving for, whether they realize it or not, because with peace comes happiness, with peace comes fulfillment, with peace comes love in all forms and in all ways. It is really peace you seek when you are looking for what has been lost. It is peace you seek when you are searching for the next best thing or setting your sights on something more, something better, but you just can't quite put your finger on it. It is peace.

Peace is the ultimate equalizer. It does not matter if you are rich or poor, what color your skin is, what religion you practice, or even if you don't practice at all. Peace is available to everyone. Peace is possible for everyone. With all the talk about peace in the world, doesn't it make sense to have peace individually first? Do you not think that if all the world's leaders had peace in their own souls, they would put an end to war?

When peace is in individuals, then peace is in families. When peace is in families, then peace is in communities. When peace is in communities, then peace in cities. When peace is in cities, then peace is in states. When peace is in states, then peace is in countries. When peace is in countries, then peace will be in the world. When there is peace in the world, there will be peace on the planet. When there is peace on the planet, then the universe will stop trying to get human attention, be it with natural disasters or famine or strife. There will be no need. There will be peace, and all will be well.

It sounds so simple, but it is true. If each and every human on the planet searched for peace within and worked toward that all-encompassing goal, there would be peace on the planet. Peace is possible one person at a time; peace is possible one soul at a time. Peace is possible. Peace is possible in your soul. Today. Begin today to find peace, inner peace.

How, you ask? Peace comes from forgiveness, peace comes from letting go of the past, peace comes with understanding the past so that you can release it, peace comes with forgiving yourself even more than you forgive others. Peace comes from allowing fear and all negative emotion from the past to leave so that more and more love takes its place. Peace is founded on the following acts: awareness, acceptance, understanding, ownership, and forgiveness of self. It begins and ends with you.

Be aware that you have wounds to heal, be aware that there is more to you, more for you in this life. Accept your perfect imperfections and strive to understand the whys of your decisions, even those decisions you may regret. Own each thought, feeling, word, action, reaction, and any that hurt yourself or others or both. Ownership can be difficult, because there is no victim when you own what you said or didn't say, what you did or didn't do, and you look at who you were with awareness, acceptance, and understanding, and you own it all. Then you will find the compassion to forgive who you were then and finally be at peace with yourself. Then, finding peace within yourself, you will look at others with more acceptance and understanding and will begin to see your place in how to bring peace to others, and so it goes, and so it goes. Peace: it is possible, it is probable, it is yours.

Elizabeth Pelkey

Reflection

Resilience

❖ ❖ ❖

WHAT DOES IT mean to be resilient? What does it mean to survive? They are one and the same, really. To be resilient is to survive, plain and simple. You will find a way, some way, to move through something, to work through something, to endure something, to eventually survive that something. Why, then, do so many think they do not have what it takes? Why, then, do so many think and feel that they are not worthy, when each and every human being on the planet has worth?

This self-worth brings about the belief that not only can one make it through, that one can survive, but that one can thrive as well. Live a full and peaceful life. More struggle in one's life does not necessarily mean one is more resilient, because each individual soul requests different lessons. So, if you have endured many struggles in your lifetime and have not only endured or survived, but also are thriving or trying to thrive, then you are resilient, because what is resilience without struggle? There needs to be something that one is resilient about.

The ability to bounce back, so to speak, does not mean you have to have a lot of struggle in your life. You can bounce back from not getting the job you want or breaking up with the one you love and figure out a way to survive and eventually thrive. However, those with the greatest lessons and the most to endure don't always have resilience, and it is not that it is missing or they are without it, it is not seen. Each and every one of you has resilience inside of you. Whether you have exercised this ability or not, it is within you. You can endure, you can survive, you can thrive.

Reflection

_____

_____

_____

_____

_____

_____

_____

_____

_____

_____

_____

_____

_____

_____

_____

_____

_____

_____

_____

_____

_____

_____

_____

_____

_____

_____

_____

_____

_____

Risk

❖ ❖ ❖

RISK CAN BE viewed as either a positive or a negative. The word "risk" conjures up for some anxiety and uncertainty—what is the risk if I do this or if I don't do that? Risk is all in the eyes of the beholder, much like beauty. It is your perception of risk that is different from that of others.

Certainly there are universal risks. For example, most everyone would agree that if you step into a lion's cage, the risk to your life is great, but to the lion tamer there is minimal risk, because the lion tamer not only knows what he is doing, but also knows the risk involved and to him, it is minimal. If he does his job, his perception is that he will not be hurt or killed, but the risk is always there.

Risk is weighing the percentage of a good outcome versus a bad outcome. With great risk comes great reward, but is the reward worth the risk? Because much like the lion tamer there are risks you are willing to take, and there are risks that bring you fear. You may be afraid that if you do risk something many times, and nothing is gained, then all you will have is regret. Why not take the chance to try something new, to meet someone new, to try a new experience, go outside of your comfort zone, change your patterns of behavior and take a leap of faith? Trusting yourself, much like the lion tamer, with the knowledge you have and the faith you have in your own ability. Risk is trying something and not knowing the outcome. Risk requires faith. Faith in your own judgment, faith in your own knowledge, faith in your own feelings, faith in your own journey. To risk is to believe in yourself and take chances where the reward outweighs the potential loss.

Reflection

Seek. Search. Be Aware.

❖ ❖ ❖

LOOK AND YOU shall find that which you are looking for. So many are not willing to even start the search. Just by taking this first step, you will move forward in your soul's journey. Seek that which fills your soul with joy, fills your soul with wisdom, is true to your soul, and this truth can then be shared with others. Everyone is a seeker, but very few will actually seek that which serves their own soul and therefore the greater good. It is within each and every one of you to seek the truth, seek the wisdom, seek the joy, and then share it with those around you.

Why are you blind to what is right in front of you? Why are you afraid to look beyond the obvious to what is really there, to what is actually real, to what is necessary to change, to work on, and to heal? Why do you not want to find the truth? What about the truth scares you? What is it about the answer—finding the answer—that you fear? Why is it that you will not seek the truth? Are you afraid you will find all that you are looking for, and then what? That if there is nothing to find, the search is over?

No, the search is not over, and it never will be, because the soul is always on a journey, until the moment of your death and beyond. Your soul is always on a journey of discovery, and it is up to you to find what your soul needs in this lifetime, in this incarnation, in order to heal and grow and learn and be all that your soul set out to be. Seek and you shall find, search and you will discover truth, look and you will see beauty, sit in stillness and you will hear wisdom, search and be still, as the answers lie in the stillness—every single one. Be still. Be silent. Be aware. Be a seeker for your soul.

Reflection

Silence

❖ ❖ ❖

IN SILENCE WE hear our own soul. In silence we hear the voices of the many. In silence we hear the songs of love, the songs of joy, and the songs of unity. There is too much noise in the world, too much commotion, not enough silence, and not enough stillness. Why does everyone want to be entertained by noise? Why does everyone want to hear the sound of their own voice, or the constant sound of someone else's? Why hear the sound of the streets, the sound of electronics, the sound of the masses, the sound of fear, anger, and despair?

Silence. Silence is golden—a childhood saying that speaks volumes. Silence is golden and it is sacred. There is so much to be learned in silence, in being still, in being alone with only your own body, your own soul, your own thoughts, and then even letting the thoughts go. Let them move out of your mind like a softly flowing river. Let the thoughts that cloud your mind and, in turn, your soul go. Be open to the silence within; be open to the stillness, and to the quiet.

When all noise is gone, only the words of your higher self will come through, only the words of your guides and your angels will come through, and only the sounds of comfort, love, kindness, and truth will be heard. Silence. Be still, be silent, and be within. Do this daily for just five minutes, or longer if you are able. Sit with your soul. Be one with your soul. Be in the silence and let the silence speak. Let the words of your soul flow within you and wash you with a bright white light.

Silence: the beautiful white light that is silence. The beautiful, beautiful white light that is love, that is forgiveness, that is wholeness, that is all. White light, white glorious light, white, bright, all-consuming, and all-loving. All that can be found in silence. Surround yourself with this bright white light of love. Join us. We welcome you into our place of peace and silence. Purity and light, purity and love, purity and peace. This is silence.

Elizabeth Pelkey

Reflection

Situations. Lessons. Reality.

❖ ❖ ❖

THERE ARE SITUATIONS that occur in your everyday life that are set up by you for your soul to learn the lessons of this lifetime. Remember that you have created these situations, and you have chosen these lessons, and you have, in essence, created your reality. Every single person, both good and bad, who comes into your life is there for a reason, and every single situation that you find yourself in, good or bad, is there for a reason, and that reason is simple: to learn the lesson.

You can learn the easy way or the hard way, it is completely up to you. The reality of your life here on Earth is that it is through the toughest situations that one learns the most important lessons. There will be some pain and some suffering if lessons are not learned and reality is not perceived. One must have the perception and intuition to be aware of situations as they occur, so that one can act in the way that is best for soul growth. The growth of one's soul is always for the greater good—not just personal good, but the greater good.

Remember, all lessons are for personal growth that brings about healing, which in turns leads to growth of the greater good. Do not forget that lessons are meant to heal so that one can heal and help others. Perception is reality and reality is perception. How one views one's reality is exactly where the soul is at that moment in time.

Shift the perception and shift the reality. Know that you are not alone in this process and that there are others who are available to guide you through the situations and lessons of this lifetime. All you have to do is ask for guidance, and it will come to you.

Live through the situations of your life, learn the lessons that are laid out in front of you, and become your authentic self in the process. Do the work and reap the reward of a peaceful life. Ignore the situations, refuse to learn the lessons, and then hide behind the mask of your true self. Do not do the work and you will also reap what you sow, but it will not be peace. The situations will be harder and more painful, the lessons will still have to be learned, and you will not feel peace within. It is your choice. It is always your choice.

Reflection

Surrender

❖ ❖ ❖

SURRENDER TO THE inevitability of your soul. Surrender to the love you feel inside your soul. Surrender to the path you are to take, surrender to the path you do not know, surrender to the darkness you feel is overtaking your light, surrender to the light that is in each and every one of you.

Surrender: it is not weakness, it is not defeat, and it is not a white flag. To surrender is to become one with your soul, with your chosen path, with yourself. You are, in effect, surrendering to the very core of your being, to what has guided you all the days of your life: your soul and your soul's purpose. Many will resist this surrender, because it is frightening to let go of all control, or to seemingly let go of control.

Control is an illusion, for no one truly has control over much in this earthly life. You have the perception of control, but truly what you have is choice, and choice is vastly different from control. To surrender is to actually gain more control over your path and your life. To surrender means you are putting your life in the hands of your highest self for your greater good and the greater good of humanity.

Surrender is necessary to inner peace, because in order to find peace, you must surrender to what is best for your soul, not your ego. Your ego will fight this surrender, because to the ego surrendering is losing control, it is losing the battle, it is losing the war. Yes, war. It is war in the way your ego will keep you from the peace you seek. The ego will strike out at times when you are seemingly almost at the brink of finding just what your soul has been looking for: inner peace. The ego will snatch this peace away and sabotage your being, because your ego does not want to lose: it does not want to lose control, it is does not want to lose the battle, and it definitely does not want to lose the war, because the ego believes that if it loses, then the soul wins.

Your authentic self, the self you set out to be in this lifetime, wins. Your authentic and higher self is now in charge, in control, but your highest self knows that it is not about winning and that control is not the purpose. The purpose is to love, the purpose is to heal, the purpose is to live and walk the path of the soul. The ego, now defeated, will not be cast aside, but will be joined with the soul as an integrated self with the purpose of only the highest and greatest good. You see, in surrendering there is no loser, there is no winner, there is just peace. Inner peace and love. Surrender to your highest self, surrender to the greater good, surrender and find peace.

Elizabeth Pelkey

Reflection

Success

❖ ❖ ❖

SUCCESS MEASURED IN material terms is vastly different from success measured in spiritual terms. It is the soul's success that will bring you peace, and peace cannot be bought or wagered or earned through traditional societal views of success.

What is success to you, really? Ask yourself: How will I feel successful? In what ways am I measuring success? In what ways am I setting myself up for failure instead of allowing myself to succeed? You see, this is it: You are in control of your own success, and you are in the way of your own success as well. So, how do you want it to be in your life? Success and failure measured by others or measured by yourself?

As you ask yourself these questions, reflect on your life thus far. Do you consider yourself a success? If so, in what ways? It is important that you recognize your successes as you see and feel them, not as others see them. Each and every one of you is a success just by being, and just by being aware enough to ask yourself the questions. In what ways am I successful? Then take the time to reflect and ask yourself what traits or talents or abilities led to the particular successes you see in your life. Some may feel you have none, but you do. You are reading this, are you not? It is simply enough that you see and feel your own success of *trying*.

The world of ego puts too much emphasis on success in monetary, power, or even bodily terms, but it is not wealth or power or attractiveness that leads to success or being successful. It is being in touch with yourself that is success. Being self-aware is being successful; being open to growth and healing, even in the smallest of ways, is being successful; being there for yourself and others is being successful; simply being human on Earth is being successful. You are successful at being human, are you not, with all the measured successes and perceived failures of a material life on Earth? Now is the time to continue to look within for the successes of the soul: kindness, compassion, and love.

Reflection

Thankfulness

— ❖ ❖ ❖ —

WHAT IS BEING thankful? Is it being grateful? Is it thanking others, or is it thanking yourself for the good work you have done? Being thankful and grateful are one in the same, however it is the *act* of being grateful, the *act* of being thankful that is key. One must be in a state of gratefulness, of thankfulness, more than one day a year. One must stay in a place of gratefulness every moment of every day of every month of every year. Gratefulness fills your heart and, in turn, fills your soul.

What are you grateful for? It could be as simple as a beautiful sunrise, a pet's kiss, or a smile from a stranger on a tough day. Or it could be as intricate as a mother's love, your health, the health of someone you love, or the love of someone who has been in your life for a minute or forever. The act of being grateful, the act of thanksgiving, is necessary to one's soul growth and must not be taken lightly. On Thanksgiving, for example, some are thankful they do not have to work, that they can stuff themselves with food and watch football on TV, or watch their families fight, reunite, and love again. This is all fine and good *one* day of the year, but it is the other 364 days that determine gratitude.

What are you truly grateful for? What, deep down, is your soul truly grateful for? Is it your breath? Is it the fact that you are able to live another day? Is it peace in your world or peace in the whole world? Is it for you alone, or is it shared with others? Is it for one man or all of mankind? You must look beyond the borders of your own life, beyond the borders of your own little world, and open your eyes to the entire world around you. Be thankful for the earth, for the universe, for all that is. Be grateful for love, divine love, the divine love within each and every being on Earth. Be thankful every day—not just today, every day. Every moment of every hour of every day, be thankful.

Elizabeth Pelkey

Reflection

Time

──── ❖ ❖ ❖ ────

THE WAIT IS long, but it is necessary. Patience is not something that comes naturally to those on Earth, but to us in spirit, a year is but a second. We do not understand time as humans do and therefore are not bound to it. Why must you rush, rush, rush everywhere and for just anything? What is so important that it cannot wait for a minute, an hour, a day? You are missing the wonders of this life on Earth by rushing to get a day over with. For what? What joy is there in living if one does not really live? What is the rush to do anything if there is not beauty found in the moment? Why is time so important when it is not time that one takes on to the other side?

It is not time, but the relationships between souls that matter. The souls that are brought into your life for a reason, that have made a contract with you to assist you on Earth. Many souls pass by, and some are even missed because of the amount of "doing." What is the rush? Why not stop and look around you and enjoy the beauty of where you are in this perfect place right now?

The beauty of now. There is beauty in now, but it is so easily destroyed by thoughts of yesterday and thoughts of tomorrow. It is the now that matters, the right now, the place you are at this very moment that matters more than life itself. What is a life but a tapestry of moments woven together over time? One moment, two moments, three, and so on add up in your day, but how many count? How many do you actually remember? How many moments are truly about you?

About your path? About your soul? How many moments contain the important souls in this life, the important lessons of this life, and the important beginnings of the next life? What seeds are planted? What actions are worthwhile? What souls are healed? What answers are sought? What questions go unasked?

What happens in these tiny moments is bigger than the whole of your entire earthly life. Stop rushing, stop doing, and stop wasting time. Make the moments matter. Make them matter to your soul and to those around you. The mattering of moments is the key to your happiness, and ultimately your peace.

Reflection

Truth

❖ ❖ ❖

WHY ARE so many afraid to not only speak the truth, but to live truth-
fully? Truth is being authentic to who you really are, your authentic
self. Truth is living daily in your own skin, in your own soul, as you are
meant to live. Truth is being true to the goodness within and being the
person you are deep down inside, but many hide it from others. Why
hide who you are? Because you are afraid? Because you feel others will
not understand you? Because you think others will hurt you if they
know your true soul?

It takes vulnerability and courage to be authentic and to live an
authentic life. It makes others nervous to be around those living in
truth if they are not yet aware of their own truth or are hiding from
the truth within. Pay attention to those around you who are drawn
to your truth and your light, as they are your true allies, your true
friends. If you can be completely open and 100 percent your true
authentic self, then you will be at peace and you will have joy. If you
pretend to be something you are not, then the persons you are pretending for are not part of your true life, your true soul circle, and are
not worthy of you.

Why spend time worrying what others think and what others will
like instead of going deep within and discovering what you really like,
what you really want, and who you really are? Look within, live within,
live your own truth, not someone else's version of truth. To be true is
to be alive in your own soul, to be at peace in your own soul, to know

the truth within. Does this not sound better than pretending? Than hiding? Than being false with others and with yourself?

Then free yourself from a self-imposed lie and be true to your beliefs, be true to your nature, be true to your soul. The gift of truth is one of the greatest gifts you can give yourself. It is authentic. It is real. It is not manmade. It is divine. It is light. It is love. Love your authentic self, and do not fear sharing this self with the world. It is who *you* really are, it is your truth, it is your divine light, it is *you*.

Elizabeth Pelkey

Reflection

_____
_____
_____
_____
_____
_____
_____
_____
_____
_____
_____
_____
_____
_____
_____
_____
_____
_____
_____
_____
_____
_____
_____
_____
_____
_____
_____

Truth (Part Two)

❖ ❖ ❖

Is it so hard to tell the truth? Is it so hard to listen to the truth? Is it so hard to face the truth within your own soul? Yes, it is hard, and many times the truth that you fear is what will heal. Truth always heals. Truth always is the best option, as when you hide from the truth, it will find you every time. Every single time, truth will win out, don't you see? Then why lie in the first place? It is unkind and unjust to lie to others, but even more so to lie to yourself.

You must be truthful to yourself. You must learn to know yourself well enough that you can face the truth within. What is so scary? That you will find out you are not perfect? Ha! No one is; every single human being who walks the earth is imperfect and makes mistakes. Every single person is walking around with a secret, something that they hide from others. It is part of human nature.

Telling the truth, however, does not mean that all truths must be shared with others, but they must be acknowledged within. You must acknowledge your truth and then grow to accept both your light and your shadow. The truths that one hides are many times the shadows within, and without facing your shadows, you can never come into the light. Release your shadows, open yourself up to the truth about yourself, and find acceptance. Then and only then will you find peace with all sides of yourself.

Everyone has shadow and everyone has light. Choose to shine your light on others. Choose to acknowledge and forgive your shadows so you can come fully into the light, where you are intended to be. In the light, in self, in truth. Be truthful to all that you are and accept all that you are. Acceptance is one step closer to a soul that is healed, to a soul that is cleansed, to a soul that is whole. Find your truth, acknowledge your truth, share your truth, and live your truth.

Reflection

Union. Communion. Togetherness.

———— ❖ ❖ ❖ ————

THERE IS A necessity to life with others, a necessity to communing with nature, being with another person or in another place. Connections made are connections that are necessary to sustain one's soul. Without this connection, one will never be completely whole or have joy. This is not to say that one must have a partner in life to be happy, to be whole, to have joy, but connections are necessary for soul growth.

After connections are made, one can choose a solitary life, but a life that is still connected in some way to other beings, other cultures, other worlds. One cannot just sit within all the time. Going within is necessary for the soul, but it is with others that we find our true purpose, our true loves, our true passions, our true self. It is reflected through the eyes and, more important, the soul. Our light reflects upon and is reflected back on us through others, as in the phrase "the eye are the windows of the soul." Let someone close enough to see inside the windows of your soul, of your being, of your light. Your light will flicker and flame and will ignite another's flame, and another's and another's, and so on and so on and so on. Do not be afraid to share your light with others, as it is your essence and it is meant to be shared.

So be in union with others, stay connected to the world, share your light, and your flame will grow brighter and brighter. Your light will bring brightness to those around you and to the world. Share your light. Be the light that shields others from darkness. Be the light that shines brightly for the world to see. Be the light that brings forth love. Love and light. Light and love. They are one and the same.

Elizabeth Pelkey

Reflection

Victory

❖ ❖ ❖

To win, to take the prize, to succeed, to beat, or to take control—however you imagine the concept of victory, know that it is about power, and this power carries with it both the negative and the positive, as when one claims victory, someone or something else must claim defeat. It is important to know what you are fighting for or against. Why is it important for you to be victorious? Is it for the greater good? Is it for the good of your soul? Is it for the good of someone close to you? For the team? For the community?

Victory for selfish purposes will never serve the soul; in fact, you may sabotage yourself by committing to a "game" that is not yours to play and claiming a victory that is not yours to win. Ask yourself: Why am I involved? What good is this for my soul, for my journey, for my path? Why is winning so important? Why does someone or something else have to lose?

What if you change your mindset away from winning and toward becoming? I will become what I need to in order to accomplish this goal. I will become what is asked for, what is expected, what is truly important. I will become humbled, I will become empowered, I will become. I will become. Becoming to your own soul. Give up the fight, give up the desire to win, give up the worry of losing, of not being enough. You are enough. You are strong. You are able. You have the power to become whatever your soul needs for growth.

Remember, sometimes these "games" of winning and losing are set before you as lessons for your soul. Will you play along? Will you get caught up in the game? Or will you stop, listen, and allow yourself to become what your soul needs without the need to be victorious, without the need to win, without the need to surpass someone else? Be satisfied with yourself, with your own progress, with your own intention, and with your own abilities. Become that which you seek to heal your soul. Become that which you seek to find your path. Become that which you seek to find peace.

Reflection

Words

❖ ❖ ❖

WORDS OF TRUTH, words of kindness, words of pain, words of love, words of shame. Words can build up or words can destroy. Words are many times more powerful than actions, because words live on in the memory long after actions have faded. Words can be heard over and over again. What words do you want to be remembered by? What words to do you want others to hear? What words do you let fall from your lips? How often is what you say not what you mean? How often do words escape your lips and you instantly wish they were back in your mouth?

Use your words wisely. Select only words of kindness and encouragement, words that will build, not break down. Words of love and charity, not words of shame and anger. It is better to be silent than to speak words that will hurt, words that will alter a relationship forever. It is not just the words you speak to others, but the words you say to yourself that are important. What do you say to yourself to encourage? What do you say to yourself to build confidence? What do you say to yourself to love? What do you say to yourself each and every day?

Use your words to help heal and bring you the peace you deserve. When you use words of love, kindness, and respect for yourself, you will undoubtedly use words of love and compassion with others. The words we share with others are only a reflection of what we feel about ourselves. Use your words to heal, to help, to comfort, to love. Use your words—not the words running through your head, but the words that come from deep within your soul. Harness the power of these words to channel all your strength and courage, and use these words to heal yourself. This is the only way to be certain that the words you share with others are pure and that they are authentic. Your words need to come from your soul, from the pureness of your soul.

Be careful; be so very careful with what you say. Words are more powerful than you can imagine. Please use your words to love and build and cherish. Eliminate words of hate, of anger, of shame, of deceit, of self-loathing. Use your words wisely. Use only words of kindness, words of compassion, words of love, words of peace, and words of light.

Elizabeth Pelkey

Reflection

Worry

❖ ❖ ❖

WHY DO YOU worry? Why do you waste precious time that can be used for living in the present worrying about the future? Why do you invest so much in an action that is useless to the mind, body, and soul? What has already happened has happened and cannot be erased. What is going to happen might change, but if you are powerless to control it, then why waste energy worrying about it?

To live in the present, to be fully *present* in the present is what is important. Do not waste your time in the past, do not worry about the future, take the time to pay attention to what is happening now. What are your actions in the present? What are your feelings in the present? What decisions are you making right now that could impact your future? This is how you prepare for but not worry about the future.

Be prepared and make sure that your *thoughts and actions are aligned.* That you are thinking and acting in accordance with your own soul. That you are thinking and acting in a way that is kind to both yourself and others. That you are thinking and acting in a way that is authentic to your soul. In order to do this, you must know who you are, and not just on the surface. In order to really know, you must go within and sit awhile with both your shadow and your light. You must know exactly who *you* are. Without this knowledge, how can you think and act in a way that is true? In a way that is right? In a way that is purposeful?

You can take the worry out of the future if you know yourself and know your purpose. How? Learn to know yourself. Spend time alone with your own thoughts. Spend time alone with your being. Understand why you behave the way you do. Understand why you think the way you do. So many are so afraid to get to know their own mind and their own soul, when this is the key to making the choices today that will have a positive effect on the future. Hence, no worry. Take the time, get to know your own soul, find your purpose, and find your peace.

Reflection

Worthiness

❖ ❖ ❖

AM I WORTHY? This is a question you ask yourself daily, even if you do not vocalize the words. Am I worthy? Some of you may think, Well, of course I am worthy, but do you act as if you are? Do you treat yourself with respect? Do your thoughts, feelings, actions, and reactions serve your soul, make you feel as though you are worthy of all the good that life can hold?

So you see, to be human is to feel doubt, to be human is to learn lessons through pain and suffering, and this pain and suffering bring about memories and feelings that all rise, from fear, doubt, shame, sadness, anger, frustration, and so on, that all keep a soul from feeling its own worth, its own value. Each and every one of you is worthy of love—it is as simple as that, and as complicated. Because to be human is to complicate that which is so very simple.

Allow the negativity from the past to be released through awareness, through forgiveness, through letting go, and with each and every negative emotion from the past released, more and more of your own self-worth can be seen. You see, it was there all along, you just haven't been able to see behind the veil of unworthiness. Questioning your very existence, questioning your choices and your reactions to your choices, questioning why you sabotage that which you know will bring happiness: this is what happens when you do not see your own worth, your own value.

We see the worth in each and every one of you. To take on a human life is the bravest act a soul can choose, because every lesson takes a little from that self-worth so that you, human, can seek to find it once again. It is not lost, it is just hidden from view, and as you clear the pain from your body, mind, and spirit, your worth and value will shine through. The light of worthiness is never extinguished; it can be dimmed but never shut out. It is eternal, you are eternal, and you are worthy and always will be.

Reflection

Daylight for the Soul is meant for anyone who wants guidance on the path of peace and love. Come back to these meditations at any time during your life as you continue your spiritual journey. Allow your spirit to be lifted by the words of love and compassion found not only on these pages, but in your own heart. Find the perfectly imperfect you each and every day and choose to embrace life from a place of love over fear to find peace within.

It is my hope that this book provides counsel in spiritual growth and helps you find inner peace. May these meditations allow for the dark night of the soul to be replaced with the light of the day ahead. There is so much to be thankful for and so much that can be felt with the heart. Living in a place of peace is possible for all.

In love and light,
Elizabeth Pelkey

About the Author

Elizabeth Pelkey spent seventeen years in marketing and then ten years teaching high-school English. During this second phase of her career, she delved into personal healing with the assistance of an energy therapist. Now her mission is to help others find inner peace.

Pelkey serves her clients as a spiritual counselor, healer, and channel through which they can communicate with their angels or spirit guides. In the words of one person who has been touched by Pelkey's gift of healing, "It's like boot camp for the soul."

Made in the USA
Monee, IL
12 February 2020